SPIRIT OF THE

DALES PONY

JACKIE SNOWDON

First published in Great Britain in 2010

British Library Cataloguing-in-Publication Data
A CIP record for this title is available from the British Library

ISBN 978 1 906887 94 0

PiXZ Books
Halsgrove House, Ryelands Industrial Estate,
Bagley Road, Wellington, Somerset TA21 9PZ
Tel: 01823 653777
Fax: 01823 216796
email: sales@halsgrove.com

An imprint of Halstar Ltd, part of the Halsgrove group of companies
Information on all Halsgrove titles is available at: www.halsgrove.com

Printed and bound in China by Toppan Leefung Printing Ltd

Introduction

Hidden away in the Northern Dales of the Upper Pennines the Dales pony has been a very well kept secret for many years.

Originally bred as a pack pony to transport 'pigs' (large ingots) of lead, it was adapted through careful crossing with a variety of breeds to become an ever-useful utility pony that is both hardy and stylish.

To look at these hairy ponies it is difficult to imagine that their origins lie in the crossing of wild native mares with quality stallions that were also influential in the development of such breeds as the Hackney, Morgan and Welsh Cob.

The people of the North knew a thing or two about ponies and through very careful infusions of new blood were able to keep the attributes of great strength and a wonderful temperament whilst fitting a pony for a range of purposes. The use of only the very best of travelling stallions on their precious mares resulted in a wonderful pony that could work all week and still be stylish and energetic enough to transport the family on Market Day.

The history of the Dales pony is closely intertwined with that of its near neighbour the Fell pony. For generations the main difference between the two breeds was one of height and whether a pony had been bred on the west or east side of the Pennine range.

By 1916 the Dales Pony Improvement Society was founded and they opened their own stud book.

The Dales became very popular with the Army buyers in the 1920s but the Second World War so very nearly saw the end of the breed. The Army continued to take many ponies and of those that remained the mares were used to produce 'vanners' or were even taken for town work. Few of these ponies came back and the breed's future was hanging in the balance.

Thankfully in its homeland a few dedicated breeders remained true to this heavy pony and by the 1960s the breed society had been reorganised, ponies actively sought out for registration and the numbers began to grow again.

Most Dales ponies alive today can trace their ancestry to the stallion Wheatside Perfect who did so much to promote the breed in the 1960s, when shown so successfully by his owner and breeder Mr T. Emerson.

Over the last twenty years its popularity has increased and the future of this breed seems assured. Although still classed as 'Endangered' by the Rare Breeds Survival Trust its numbers are closely monitored and are increasing.

The Dales Pony Society works tirelessly to ensure that the ponies remain true to type and full of quality.

These head-turning ponies are increasingly sought after. The ultimate pleasure pony, these tough characters are keen and willing to try a real range of disciplines. Whilst still seen by some as primarily a driving pony they are achieving success in many spheres, including dressage, endurance, Le Trec, showing and of course as a brilliant family pony.

Whilst not the biggest of breeds what they lack in height they make up for in character and strength and truly are 'the great all rounder'.

As the air warms up, the expectant mares begin to lose their winter coats and enjoy some welcome sunshine.

Despite the chill wind there is still a little grass to be found.

This young pony shows the intelligence and alert nature of the breed.

Right:
A well earned rest for
Sungreen Black Velvet,
who for many seasons
has hunted and competed in
Endurance rides with owner
Rebecca Harrison.

Opposite:
Spring is in the air and
even this uneven terrain
doesn't stop the fun.

Above:
Testing the air. This 'flehmen response' is
natural equine behaviour, helping them
analyse smells. It is often observed in stallions
when they are running out with mares.

Right:
Many stallions have a very busy spring.

Stallions don't always have it their own way.
This young mare expresses herself in a very determined fashion.

Left:
Eating is a favourite pastime.

Opposite:
Dales shows often spark many
friendly discussions. The Stallion Show
is held every first Saturday in May at
Barnard Castle, County Durham.

Dales Pony Society Chairman Mr Jeff Daley shares a few tender moments
with his homebred mare Highcroft Ella at the Spring Show.

Above:
Winning the Senior Stallion Class
at the Spring Show 2009.

Right:
Twywell Samuel Pepys
proudly shows off his rosette.

15

Above:
Junior stallions waiting to go in the ring.

Right:
The show gives a perfect
showcase for the breed.

Opposite:
A full range of colours line
up in the gelding class.

An impressive selection of mares wait in the ring.

Obviously pleased. It is a great accolade to win a prize at the Breed Show.

An opportunity to roll whilst baby relaxes.

Opposite: Early summer sees the birth of most foals.

It's so tiring being a foal. A chance to sleep after an exhausting first day of life.

Above:
A very proud dad. Stallions are calm and gentle, even when running out with their mares and foals.

Left:
Less than a week old this foal seeks shade and security in the silky hair of her mother's mane.

Sharing.

Above:
Grey foals are often born black
and grey out gradually over time.

Right:
There is nothing so heart warming
as a mother's love for her new baby.

Right:
Contentment.

Opposite:
Mare and foal.
Ponies keep a
watchful eye out
for anything
interesting.

Enjoying the chance to stretch her legs, this elderly mare enjoys the sunshine.

Above:
Stuffynwood Louisa-Mae celebrates
her win with owner and breeder
Mr E Hayes at the Derbyshire Dales
and Fell Show held in June.

Left:
A visit from the farrier.

As the popularity of the breed increases shows are being held throughout the country. A strong class of mares at Bakewell.

Ringside. Dales Pony
Society President Mrs
Iona FitzGerald in
conversation with
Mr Redfearn.

Face to face. High summer, foals are growing stronger and have time to enjoy their surroundings.

Relaxing together as a herd.

Herd discipline. With a strict pecking order an older mare keeps everyone in their place.

Opposite:
Although predominantly black in colour there are now an increasing numbers of roans.
The colour nearly died out in the early 1980s.

Enjoying the
freedom to run.

Milk bar time.

This young foal shows
the kind eye, which is
such a feature of
the breed.

Watching the world go by.

Opposite: Ponies on the moor can travel long distances finding food and shelter.

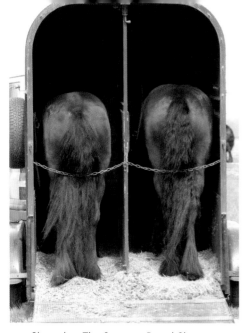

Show day. The Summer Breed Show is
held in Barnard Castle, County Durham,
on the first Saturday in August.

Ackram Rose and May Queen XI made
an impressive pair when competing at
breed shows in the 1980s.

Bolam Starlight II looks
after her 9-year-old rider
Owen Wallbanks in
the Young Rider Class.

Show Champion. Mr and Mrs D. Eccles'
mare Westwick Fashion.

Left:
Whatever the weather the show
goes on. Usually held in beautiful
sunshine, the 2009 Summer Show
proved to be rather more inclement.

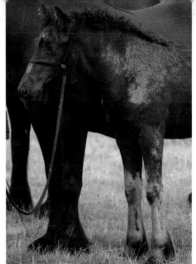

Waiting patiently in the ring.

Left:
Patience is a virtue. Calm and content this mare and foal wait for their chance to go in the ring.

Stripped for the Judge. Faradale Barney shows off his wonderful colouring. The Summer Breed Show hosts the qualifying class for the National Pony Society Mountain and Moorland Ridden Pony of the Year, held at Olympia in December.

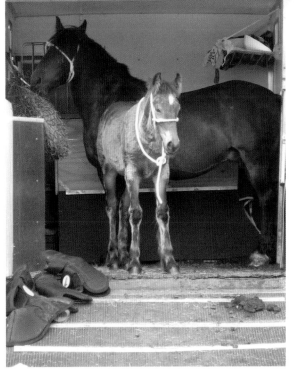

The winner. Dain Atherden and Castle Hill Flash qualify for the 2009 final at Olympia.

Left:
Waiting in the wagon.

Westwick Lizzie celebrates after winning her ridden class.

Opposite: Herd life. More often than not, the greatest passion in a Dales pony's life is eating.

A time for reflection in late August.

Right:
Sharing. Mum always knows
which is the best grass to eat.

Pingate Renegade and Lucy Bellwood jump for fun in the friendly atmosphere of the Annual Performance Show held at the end of August.

Left: The relaxed atmosphere at the Performance Show means everyone is encouraged to have a go.

Slaypits Bella celebrates at the 2009 Performance Show. This show has just celebrated its 25th Anniversary and is as popular as ever.

The Handy Pony class is always entertaining. Dales are rarely flustered by the obstacles but do treat many of them with great suspicion.

Working hunter classes are always popular.

Despite being partially sighted, Hillbro Matilda trusts her owner Frances Reeds enough to compete in jumping classes. The pair are regulars at the Annual Performance Show, competing in the Open section.

Being inquisitive is so important!

Making the most of the autumn sunshine.

Mother and son. As winter nears owners keep a watchful eye on the ponies, providing mineral blocks to ensure the mares retain their condition.

A quiet life.

Autumn sees the Ploughing Match season. Countrylane Gemma and Countrylane Beauty competed in numerous Ploughing Matches during the early 2000s.

Ploughing pair in action.

Left:
November sees the Annual
Foal Show, held at the Auction
Mart in Barnard Castle,
County Durham.

Opposite:
Gathering together. The Society
organises rides for members
through Area groups.
These are always well supported
and are a wonderful sight.

Swayfield Amy prepares
for the ride.

Setting off on a winter's ride through Chatsworth Park in Derbyshire.

Even on the coldest of days, Dales ponies prove themselves to be a strong and hardy breed.

Walls provide excellent shelter when the weather turns cold.